Direct Care and Security Staff
Trainee Handout

Limit & Lead:
Behavior Management Training Program

Matthew L. Ferrara, Ph. D.
2500 West William Cannon Drive Austin, TX 78745
Telephone: (512) 708-0502   Fax: (512) 708-0557
mferraraphd@att.net
http://www.doctorferrara.com

Direct Care and Security Staff Trainee Handout
Limit & Lead: Behavior Management Training Program

Table of Contents

The Role of Behavior Management

Behavior management consists of everything that you do to prevent youths from acting out. The key idea in this definition is *prevention*. Anything that you do to prevent acting out is behavior management.

There are many different ways for you to do behavior management. Consider the following list of behavior management interventions:

- Huddle-ups
- Praise
- Informal discussions
- Behavior groups

- Large groups
- Outings
- Consequences and rewards
- Levels

In residential programs for conduct disordered youths, behavior management is the foundation. If the youths do not feel safe, no rehabilitation can occur. The hierarchy below shows the different levels of intervention. Notice that behavior management is a Level One intervention. In other words, behavior management is the foundation for all other parts of a residential program.

<u>Type of Intervention</u>		<u>Result</u>
Level Three: **Specialized Treatment** Interventions for specific issues such as sexual abuse trauma, aggression control, and capital offending	→	Treatment
Level Two: **Rehabilitation** Services designed to reduce reoffending	→	Rehabilitation
Level One: **Behavior Management** Interventions designed to prevent acting out	→	Basic safety and security

1

Before a program can rehabilitate conduct disordered youths, the facility must be safe. Youths cannot be allowed to worry about whether they will get assaulted while addressing and working toward resolving personal issues. Each youth must know that he or she will not be harmed at the facility and that he or she will not be allowed to hurt anyone else there. Rehabilitation can take place only after a safe environment has been created.

Behavior management is the most fundamental part of any program. If behavior management is ineffective, nothing else in the program will work.

The Research Basis of Behavior Management

As a behavior management professional, you have the most critical job in any facility for conduct disordered youths. You are responsible for creating and maintaining a safe environment. Without safety, rehabilitation is impossible.

The behavior management approach described in this manual is based on many years of research with conduct disordered youth. This research clearly shows that conduct disordered youths have specific characteristics and that they respond positively to certain kinds of help. This research tends to focus on three primary areas, each of which is listed below.

Population: Conduct Disordered Youth

- The juvenile delinquent triad (i.e., entitlement, power play, and selfishness)
- The two-factor theory (i.e., rebelliousness and thrill-seeking)

Problem: Conduct disordered youth Behavior

- Crime is an interpersonal interaction. When conduct disordered youth act out, someone gets hurt. We must always remember the victim.
- Since conduct disordered youths have developed exquisite delinquent skills, they have not developed citizen skills.
- Conduct disordered youths will establish a delinquent environment in a facility or group, unless it is prevented or confronted.

Interventions: Rehabilitation

- Rehabilitation services are interventions designed to reduce the likelihood of new criminal activity. Treatment services are interventions designed to help youths overcome psychological problems.
- *Research has identified effective rehabilitation approaches*, including family therapy with parental skills training, token economies that reward prosocial behavior, behavioral contracting, role-playing to teach citizenship skills, guided group interaction, prevocational and vocational skills training, training to alter conduct

disordered youth thinking, training to alter thinking about specific problems (e.g., substance abuse, violence, and deviant sex), social skills education, and role-playing involving social skills.

- *Research has also identified ineffective rehabilitation approaches*, including nondirective approaches, self-help groups that are not monitored by staff, deterrence, failure to neutralize support for delinquent behavior, ignoring why the conduct disordered youth was recommended for the program, Freudian-based therapies, friendship models, punitive approaches, psychotropic therapy, and individual therapy.

- Effective rehabilitation specialists possess certain characteristics.

The Limit & Lead Behavior Management Approach

You have just learned some characteristics of conduct disordered youths and their behavioral tendencies. You have also learned about effective and ineffective rehabilitation approaches. Nevertheless, you might be confused about what this means for your job. How can this information help you supervise, manage, and control the youths you will be responsible for?

All of the information that you just learned can be used to define your job. In the left column is all the information discussed in the previous lesson. In the right column you will find a description of how you can use that information to do your job.

Conduct disordered youth Behavior, Characteristics, and Rehabilitation Approaches	How to Use This Information
The juvenile delinquent triad (i.e., entitlement, power play, and selfishness)	**Confront** acts of power seeking, entitlement, and selfishness
The two factor theory (i.e., rebelliousness and thrill-seeking)	**Confront** rebellion and **teach** ways of avoiding boredom.
Interpersonal nature of crime	**Confront** the victimizer when he or she tries to victimize you or anyone else. **Teach** victim empathy.
Highly efficient delinquent skills	**Confront** the use of these skills.
Creating a delinquent environment on the dorm	**Confront** the organization of any delinquent environment.
Lack of citizen skills	**Teach** social skills.
Use of delinquent thinking	**Teach** the attitudes, values, and beliefs of citizenship.
A passive or friendly approach; or a harsh or punitive approach does not work	**Confront** and **teach** by being a professional with clear boundaries who is neither harsh nor weak.

As shown in the above table, there are really only two things that you do: *confront* and *teach*. The Limit & Lead Behavior Management Program is a two-step process that involves *confronting* and *teaching*. Both components of the approach are necessary: doing one without the other will lead to failure.

In your position, seek out ways to confront and teach. As per your job duties, you will be waking up youth, taking them to school or the infirmary, or monitoring them in the dorm. In all of these interactions you will have to supervise the youth. But as you supervise, you must also watch for any opportunities to confront or teach.

Your Job: Confront and Teach

Confront and teach is another way of saying *limit and lead*. To do your job correctly, you must be able to confront and teach. The best intervention that you can have with a conduct disordered youth is any one in which you confront and teach during the same interaction. In such an interaction, you basically tell the youth, "Don't do that (i.e., confront). Do this instead (i.e., teach)."

You confront when you put limits on harmful behavior. Some of the things you should and shouldn't do when confronting are listed below.

When You Confront, You Should:	When You Confront, You Should *Not*:
• Confront only destructive behavior.	• Don't confront by raising your voice.
• Confront sooner rather than later.	• Don't confront by using put-downs.
• Confront before you teach.	• Don't confront by insulting.
• Be prepared to teach if the confrontation is successful.	• Don't confront by attacking the youth's personality.
• Teach as you confront.	• Don't confront by attacking the youth's ability.

Some *good* confrontations are:

- "What could you do instead of that?"
- "Stop!"
- "You need to move your chair over to that table."
- "You are not lined up properly. Please get in line."

Some *bad* confrontations are:

- "Hey stupid. You know better than that."
- "You always screw-up. Cut it out."
- "What kind of person are you?"

Teaching refers to leading youth in prosocial directions. Some things to remember while teaching are listed below.

When You Teach, You Should:	When You Teach, You Should *Not*:
• Only expect the youth to use the positive skills that you have taught him or her.	• Don't assume that the youth knows what to do.
• Break complex behaviors into smaller components.	• Don't assume the youth understands your vocabulary.
• Teach prosocial behaviors (i.e. of citizenship).	• Don't assume the youth understands your explanation.
• Teach prosocial values (i.e., of citizenship).	• Don't assume the youth can figure out the details.
• Teach prosocial ways of solving problems (i.e., citizenship).	• Don't blame the youth for not knowing what to do.

Some *good* examples of teaching are:

- "If you want to succeed, you need to do this first, then this, and then this."
- "I notice you keep having trouble in school. Have you thought about doing this?"

Some *bad* examples of teaching are:

- "Do it right."
- "If you would just pay attention, you wouldn't have these problems."

Confrontation is aimed only at the behavior, not the person. Confrontation is used to limit the youth's ability to meet his or her needs at the expense of others. If you limit behavior other than conduct disordered youth behavior, then you are not doing your job. You are probably carrying out a personal agenda, not performing your job. For example, you might initiate a confrontation because you are frustrated about personal problems at home, with finances, or with your own children.

Teaching interventions instruct youth to be citizens. Most importantly, teaching interventions teach youth how to meet their needs in the manner of citizens.

Some individuals who work with conduct disordered youth think all they really need to do is teach. This is wrong. A youth is not motivated to learn a new social skill until he or she is confronted and cutoff from using acting out behavior to meet his or her needs. Confrontation cuts off the youth's ability to meet his or her needs by exploiting others. Teaching shows the youth a way to meet his or her needs without harming another person. Taken together, confronting and teaching form a total system for building a safe environment and helping youth to develop the attitudes and behaviors of citizens.

Active Listening

Your job begins with listening. When you listen well, you not only hear what a youth is saying but also notice how he or she is saying it. How a youth says something is often more important than what he or she says.

Listening

To listen, you should use active-listening skills. Active listening means paying close attention to not only what a person says but how the person says it. You need to do three things when to successfully apply basic active-listening skills:

1. **Maintain eye contact:** Do not stare but do look into the speaker's eyes. Make enough eye contact so that the person knows that you are listening, but do not make so much eye contact that you lose track of your job: to supervise all of youth assigned to you.

2. **Observe nonverbal cues**: Be aware of nonverbal cues, including tone of voice, rate of speech, and gestures. Ask yourself a few questions as you listen:

   - Is this the youth's normal rate of speech?
   - Does this youth's voice appear to be at a normal pitch?
   - What kind of gestures is the youth making?
   - Are the gestures that the youth is making consistent with what he or she is saying?
   - Does the youth's overall behavior communicate a message?
   - *Intuition*: How do I feel as the youth speaks to me?

By asking yourself these questions, you can remind yourself of the nonverbal behaviors that you must consider. You should especially watch for one type of verbal behavior: slips of the tongue.

3. **Tracking:** As the speaker talks, absorb the information communicated by making a mental list of the major points or by keeping a mental summary of what the speaker is saying.

The goal of active listening is twofold: to know what the speaker said and to have some idea about why the speaker is saying these things. You must both understand the content of the speaker's message and understand why the speaker is communicating the particular message at this particular time.

Role-Playing

Pair-up with another trainee and use the role-play scenarios below. One trainee should play the role of the youth while the other should use active listening. The trainee playing the youth should talk for a few minutes and then stop. While role-playing, the trainee using active listening skills should *not respond* but *only listen*.

After role-play stops, the trainee who used active listening should summarize what he or she heard and observed, including eye contact, nonverbal cues, and main points communicated. Both trainees should then switch roles and repeat the activity. Use the role-play scenarios listed below.

Role-Playing Scenarios

1. A youth just received a letter from home and is really upset. In the letter, the mother tells the youth that she lost both her job and her apartment. (*Note*: The youth is truly worried about the mother and wants to find a way to send her money.)

2. A youth just received a letter from home and is really upset. In the letter, the mother tells the youth that she lost both her job and her apartment. (*Note*: The youth is merely trying to engage staff in a conversation so that his or her peers can go into a restricted area.)

3. A new youth arrives at the unit. During a break in the schedule, you have time to talk to this youth. You ask the youth about his or her background. (*Note*: The youth is afraid because he or she is new to the facility.)

4. A new youth arrives at the unit. During a break in the schedule, you have time to talk to this youth. You ask the youth about his or her background. (*Note*: The youth has been in many facilities and is institutionalized. The youth lies and exaggerates how bad his or her upbringing really was.)

Constructive Responding

After you have listened, you should have a good idea of what the youth is saying and why he or she said it. Then you must respond. Just as the youth communicates with verbal and nonverbal cues, so do you. You must recognize, monitor, and control your verbal and nonverbal cues if you seek to communicate effectively.

Responding

When you respond, you will respond with verbal and nonverbal cues. Consider the possible aspects of these cues as described in the lists below.

Verbal Cues	Nonverbal Cues
• **Content:** The content of your response should suit the conversation. You should talk about what the youth is talking about. • **Vocabulary:** Only use words that youth will understand. Do not talk above a youth by using complex terms. Do not use street language or cussing. Remember that your job is to teach. One way that you teach youth how to be citizens is to model how a citizen talks.	• **Tone:** The tone of your voice expresses emotion. Your tone should not sound frightened, angry, or out of control. • **Rate**: Do not talk too fast, or the youths will think that you are not calm. • **Gestures:** Do not use aggressive or obscene gestures. Do not use gang signs or gestures that could be confused with gang signs. • **Contradictions:** Make sure that your nonverbal and verbal behaviors are consistent.

Depending on what you hear, you must respond. Your two chief response options are either to confront or to teach: *if what you hear is maladaptive, you must confront and if what you hear is prosocial, you can respond by teaching.*

When you respond, consider assuming a social role that helps youth. Of the variety of roles from which you could choose, consider using one or a combination of the following when interacting with a youth or group of youth:

- **Cheerleader:** When youth are doing the right thing, you cheer them on by complimenting them and praising their behavior.
- **Coach:** You motivate and teach by getting a youth's attention. You tell a youth what he or she is doing wrong as well as how he or she can improve. As you are providing instruction, you also encourage, cajole, and motivate.
- **Confessor:** You listen in a supportive and nonjudgmental way. By accepting what a youth is saying, you provide emotional support.
- **Cop:** If a youth is acting out, it is your job to stop him or her. You must get the youth's attention and confront his or her behavior in order to successfully redirect the youth away from acting out.

You should be aware that as a staff member, some roles will come naturally while others will not. However, you should force yourself to assume roles that you are not accustomed to and likely not comfortable with. Only by rehearsing these roles will you build your response skills. The staff member who plays the most roles is the staff member who can help the most youth.

Role-Playing Scenarios

You should recognize these role-play scenarios. You will be doing the same role-play done while practicing active listening. This time, however, you will need to respond instead of only listening.

As in the first role-play activity, trainees should form pairs. One trainee will play the staff member, while the other will play the youth. When role-playing is complete, spend some time debriefing or discussing with the trainer. Then, switch roles and perform the scenario again. Be sure to debrief, or discuss, your experience after each scenario.

Each role-play scenario should last from 3 to 5 minutes. At the conclusion of each scenario, you need to discuss five things. The first three things that you will discuss focus on active listening, while the last two focus on responding.

Cover these topics when you debrief:

1) Discuss eye contact with the youth and whether you were able to watch what was happening in the room and maintain eye contact.
2) Discuss the youth's nonverbal behavior.
3) Discuss the main points of what the youth communicated.
4) Discuss the role, or roles, that you played (i.e., coach, cheerleader, cop, and confessor).
5) Discuss whether the role you played suited the situation.

1. A youth just received a letter from home and is really upset. In the letter, the mother tells the youth that she lost both her job and her apartment. (*Note*: The youth is truly worried about the mother and wants to find a way to send her money.)
2. A youth just received a letter from home and is really upset. In the letter, the mother tells the youth that she lost both her job and her apartment. (*Note*: The youth is merely trying to engage staff in a conversation so that his peers can go into a restricted area.)
3. A new youth arrives at the unit. During a break in the schedule, you have time to talk to this youth. You ask the youth about his or her background. (*Note*: The youth has been in many facilities and is institutionalized. The youth lies and exaggerates how bad his or her upbringing really was.)
4. A new youth arrives at the unit. During a break in the schedule, you have time to talk to this youth. You ask the youth about his or her background. (*Note*: The youth is afraid because he or she is new to the facility.)

When and How to Set Limits

At the first sign of acting out, you should set limits. Acting out behavior can take many forms, including not complying with staff directions, not complying with program rules, intimidating peers, threatening staff members, destroying property, and assaulting others.

There are different ways to set limits. The way that you use to set any limit should match the intensity of the youth's misbehavior. In the continuum below, the behaviors listed above the line are behaviors typical of conduct disordered youths. Appropriate staff responses for the corresponding behaviors are listed under the line. Consider how the staff response matches the behavior.

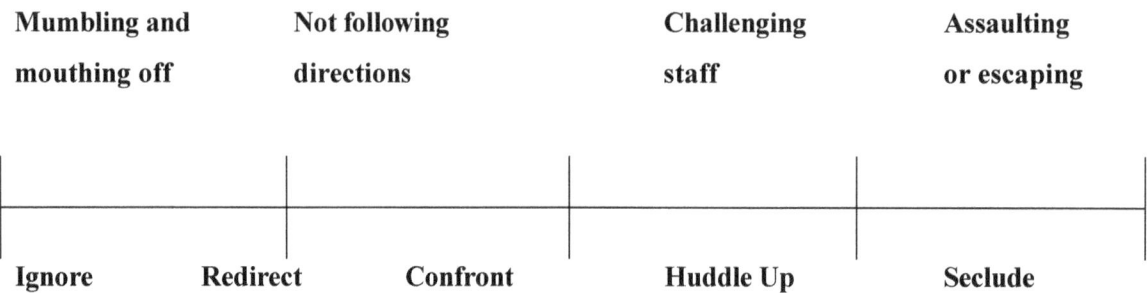

Mumbling and mouthing off	Not following directions	Challenging staff	Assaulting or escaping

Ignore	Redirect	Confront	Huddle Up	Seclude

Only a few of the limit-setting behaviors you can use are listed in the above continuum. A complete list of limit-setting interventions that staff members typically use appears on the following page.

The continuum displayed above is useful, since it can help you to visualize how to match your response to the behavior shown by the youth. As shown in the continuum, you cannot simply adopt one way of responding to the youth you supervise. On the contrary, you must adapt each response to suit the behavior in any given situation. In short, you must be flexible. If a youth shows you mild acting-out behavior, your response should be a mild intervention. If a youth exhibits severe misconduct, you should use a more vigorous intervention.

You should confront sooner rather than later. When you confront early, you can avoid more vigorous and more disruptive interventions. As a result, the youth can respond to minimal cues and change his or her behavior without losing face. Plus, less vigorous interventions are also less taxing on you.

Understand that youth most often gradually build up to exhibiting severe forms of misconduct. If a staff member can recognize and confront the potential for this build-up at the first sign of acting out, it may be unnecessary to use more vigorous ways of confronting.

If you realize that you always use very vigorous interventions, you are probably not intervening early enough and may be out of touch with the youth. Always look for ways to intervene early with mild interventions.

A good approach is to view every seclusion or restraint as a failure. Specifically, if you have to restrain a youth or send a youth to security, view this as your failure to recognize that the youth was building up to this and you didn't confront soon enough.

Finally, it is important that you learn as many limit-setting interventions as you can. *The staff person with most interventions wins!*

Definitions of Techniques for Setting Limits

You can limit misbehavior in several ways. Remember that you should match your limit-setting intervention to the severity of the misconduct. If you realize that you are frequently using very intense interventions (e.g., seclusion), you may not be recognizing the need for an intervention when a youth is building up to severe misconduct.

Severity of Acting Out	Intervention	Definition or Example
Mild misconduct	Structure of environment	You structure the environment by deciding to stand, sit, or walk while monitoring youth.
	Ignore	Not paying attention to the behavior.
	Nonverbal cues	Use a look, gesture, or hand movement to remind the youth to behave. You can even stand close to the youth who is noncompliant or misbehaving.
	Prompt	Repeat your instructions to a youth or use nonverbal cues to remind the youth of what is expected.
	Redirect	Tell a youth to stop acting out and follow the rules.
	Positive anchor	Remind the youth of past successes, and encourage the youth to use the feeling of success as the basis for doing the right thing.
Moderate misconduct	Self-directed timeout	The youth has the option of taking a self-directed timeout.
	Directive statement	Point out the misconduct and tell the youth to stop. Offer the youth two alternatives to the misconduct.
	Huddle-up	Use peer pressure to stop a problem.
	Directed timeout	Direct the youth to go to timeout.
	Consequence	Give a consequence for misconduct.

Severity of Acting Out	Intervention	Definition or Example
Major misconduct	Expulsion	A youth's behavior is chronically noncompliant or threatening, so you remove him or her from the situation.
	Large group	Convene all members of the dorm for a group discussion that focuses on accountability and problem-solving.
	Escort	If the youth is a danger to him or herself or others or may damage property, escort him or her to the timeout room.
	Therapeutic hold	Physically restrain the youth's ability to move.
	Seclusion or locked seclusion	Remove the youth from the community. Place the youth in the timeout room and lock the door.

Directive Statements

The directive statement is a crossroads. It is the technique used after ignoring, repeating, and redirecting have failed. It is the technique that you use before having to use more restrictive forms of limit setting. A good directive statement happens in several steps.

1. **Pre-confrontation gut check:** Before you use a directive statement, ask yourself three questions: (1) "What am I feeling right now?" (2) "What does this youth need or want?" and (3) "How can I best respond to this situation?" Make sure you can perform the confrontation without escalating the situation or being harsh. If you cannot issue a directive statement without escalating the situation, hand off the youth to another staff member. If you decide to perform the confrontation, take time to consider the youth's motive for misconduct. A youth's motive often suggests a solution. For example, if a youth is acting out because of bad news from home, you can talk about home to defuse the situation.

2. **Get the youth's attention:** Move closer to the youth, but do not invade his or her personal space. (At the same time, do not conduct confrontations from across the room.) When you have moved closer, tell that youth there is a problem that needs to stop. Be sure to monitor your nonverbal behavior. Do not use threatening nonverbal cues, but do not use weak or timid nonverbal cues either. Watch your tone of voice, posture, gestures, and body space.

3. **Confront the behavior:** Identify and describe the problematic behavior. Tell the youth that the behavior is disruptive, inappropriate, and needs to stop. Do not attack a youth's personality or ability or use toxic phrases, such as "You never do anything right" or "You are worthless."

4. **Ask the youth what he or she needs:** Asking what the youth needs is difficult. You may already think that you are in a power struggle with a youth. At the same time, you may think that, if you ask this question, then you will be giving into the youth's demands. If you have these thoughts, then it is time to hand off the confrontation to another staff member. When you ask a youth what he or she needs, you are the one in control. By asking this question, you change the entire situation. No longer is the problem an issue of behavioral compliance but an issue of what is going on inside a youth. This question can catch a youth off guard, and when a youth is off guard, he or she can more easily be controlled.

5. **Respond to the youth's needs:** If the youth's expressed need is unrealistic, help him or her to reframe the need, e.g., "I want to punch my roommate in the nose." Sometimes you need to help youth in setting realistic goals and expectations, e.g., "I need to tell my roommate to stop signing so much." If you are able to transform an unrealistic need into a realistic one, come up with a plan to help the youth address that need.

6. **Redirect:** After the underlying issue of the youth's misconduct has been addressed, you should redirect the youth by telling him or her that it is time to become involved in programming again. You should encourage his or her commitment to follow programming. It is usually best to offer a youth at least two options for reintegrating into the program. This way, the youth will save face and have less need to struggle for power.

Role-Playing: Scenarios for Setting Limits

Pair up with another trainee. One of you will play the youth, while the other will play the staff member. Each scenario should last from 1 to 2 minutes. When you are finished, switch roles.

1. It is time to line up to leave the room. All of the youth are lined up except one. You must get the youth in line. (*Role-play guideline*: The youth is not lining up because he or she wants to embarrass the staff member and undermine his or her authority.)

2. It is time to line up to leave the room. All of the other youth are lined up except one. You must get the youth in line. (*Role-play guideline*: The youth is not lining up because he or she fears that upon getting back to the dorm, several peers will jump him or her.)

3. You are monitoring the day area. It is loud, and youth seem to be everywhere. They are not sitting at the tables, as they are supposed to. You address the entire group and tell them to get back to their seats and quiet down. One youth shouts out, "F--- you." (*Role-play guideline*: This youth is a strong negative leader. He or she does not think that you can control him or her and has lots of negative followers.)

21

4. You are monitoring the day area. It is loud, and youth seem to be everywhere. They are not sitting at the tables, as they are supposed to. You address the entire group and tell them to get back to their seats and quiet down. One youth shouts out, "F--- you." (*Role-play guideline*: The youth is ADHD. He tends to act without thinking. He is obviously embarrassed that he just blurted out these cuss words.)

5. A table of youth in the dayroom is being loud and distracting. Other youth have checked the table, but the noise continues. You go to the table to confront the noisy youth. (*Role-play guideline*: The youth are bored and conduct disordered youth.)

6. You are distributing snacks when you see a larger youth glare at a smaller one. The smaller youth looks scared and gives his snack to the larger one. You decide to confront the larger peer. (*Role-play guideline*: The larger youth is slick and does not want to admit to any wrongdoing.)

7. You are in the gym, where a basketball game is getting increasingly rough. Youth on each team begin to threaten each other, and you suspect that it will escalate into a fight. You decide to intervene before the fight starts. (*Role-play guideline*: The teams were selected along gang and racial lines.)

When and How to Lead

There are two very good times to lead by teaching. First, you should teach immediately after you confront. Remember that your job is to confront *and* teach. Second, you should teach when a youth is receptive. Signs that a youth might be receptive to teaching are when he or she is calm, quiet, working on issues, or trying to deal with an issue. If you catch a youth doing something right, teach the youth that what he or she is doing is good.

Teaching can be done in a variety of ways. The teaching technique that you chose should suit the situation.

Least
Directive

Most
Directive

| | Supporting | Role modeling | Teaching values, beliefs, or attitudes | Problem-solving |

| | Approving | Helping with hurdles | Giving directions | Teaching emotions |
| Interpreting | | | |

As shown above, teaching techniques can be placed along a continuum from least to most directive. A less directive teaching technique does not involve directing the youth or telling the youth what to do. By contrast, a directive technique involves telling the youth what to do. The most directive form of teaching involves telling the youth what to think or feel.

It may seem odd to think that teaching can entail telling a youth how to think or feel. However, it is not odd when you realize that these youths are trying to change from being delinquents to citizens. Since youth have little-to-no experience with the thoughts and feelings of citizens, you must train, or teach, the youth in these matters.

Definitions and Techniques for Leading

By now you know that there is more than one way to teach. Teaching should match a particular youth's need(s). If a youth is already doing the right thing, all you need do is approve or support. However, if a youth is struggling with an issue, you might have to practice problem-solving.

Situation	Technique	Definition or Example
The youth is doing the right thing.	Supporting	• This is behind-the-scene intervention, since you support the youth in team meetings or staffing.
	Approving	• Tell the youth that he or she is doing well; use praise and positive reinforcement.
The youth is motivated to do well but needs guidance.	Role modeling	• Do the right thing and let the youth learn by observation.
	Helping with hurdles	• If the youth is having difficulty completing a task, you offer to help so that he or she can complete the task.
	Giving directions	• Tell a youth how to behave prosocially.
	Teaching problem-solving	• Teach a youth how to figure out the right thing to do.
The youth has little awareness or insight about what to do.	Teaching values, beliefs, or attitudes	• Teach the youth prosocial values, attitudes, and beliefs.

	Teaching emotions	• Teach the youth how to recognize, label, and control his or her feelings.
	Problem-solving	• Help the youth solve a problem; use the why sandwich to help the youth to solve an emotional problem.
	Interpreting	• Tell the youth what his or her motive was.

Teaching Emotions

There are four basic emotions: happiness, sadness, anger, and fear. Though there are more than four words for emotions, all emotions are related to one of the four basic emotions listed below.

- **Happiness:** This is a pleasant emotion. You usually feel happy when you get something that you want or when things go your way. You feel good when you are happy. You are drawn to things that make you happy.
- **Sadness:** This is an unpleasant emotion. When you feel sad, you are blue, depressed, or unhappy. You usually feel sad when you lose something or when things do not go how you had hoped.
- **Anger:** This is an unpleasant emotion. Anger is the result of being hurt. You cannot feel anger unless you first feel hurt. When you feel anger, you feel the need to take action.
- **Fear:** This is an unpleasant emotion. When you feel fear, you can be worried, anxious, or even panicky. Fear happens when you are threatened. Threats can be real or imaginary. When you feel fear, you become withdrawn, and you want to hide.

It is important to always keep in mind that there are only four emotions. Do not be fooled by all of the synonyms for emotions in the thesaurus. All words describing emotions can be traced to one of the four basic emotions listed above. Also, do not be fooled by all of the feelings you get. Each feeling is one of the above four emotions, even when your feelings are confusing. There are two good things about having only four basic emotions.

First, your job of recognizing your emotions becomes easier if you only have to determine which of the four above emotions you are feeling. Once you know that there are only four basic emotions, your emotions will be less confusing.

Second, the job of communicating your emotions becomes easier once you know that you only have to talk about one of four basic emotions. Other people can relate to you more easily when you talk about your emotions if you refer to these four.

There are three basic ways to express emotions: as an infant, as a child, and as an adult. Once you become a teenager, you are expected to express emotions as an adult.

Infants, children, and adults all have the same emotions, but the way they express emotions differs. The table below shows three ways to express emotions.

	Infant Response	Child Response	Adult Response
Happiness	Laughs uncontrollably and is reckless	Becomes giddy and inappropriate	Laughs and smiles
Sadness	Becomes severely depressed and completely hopeless	Becomes blue and unresponsive	Becomes blue and cries
Anger	Expresses rage and assaults physically	Cusses and assaults verbally	Becomes irked and irritated
Fear	Becomes panicked and cannot move	Expresses paranoia and is high strung	Becomes bothered and gets butterflies in the stomach

One final word on emotions: everyone can and does regress to childlike and infantile emotions. Sometimes the regression is maladaptive. For example, let's say that your team just won a championship. You are likely going to feel giddy and might even feel euphoria. By contrast, suppose a loved one dies. You will likely feel depressed for a while. Even though we strive for adult functioning, everyone will occasionally regress.

Hints for Teaching Emotions

1. Teach youth the four basic emotions. Tell a youth there are these emotions and no others. Tell the youth you will expect him or her to know these basic emotions.

2. When you ask a youth what he or she is feeling, ask them to respond to the question with a one-word response of one of the four emotions. When you ask the youth what he or she is feeling, expect a response such as, "It's not fair" or "No one likes me." Require the youth to use one of the four emotions to label the feeling.

3. When dealing with anger, tell a youth that he or she cannot be angry without first being hurt. Explain to the youth that, if he or she can deal with the hurt, the anger will soon go away.

4. After a youth demonstrates skills in labeling the four emotions, teach the youth how to recognize the three levels of each emotion.

The Why Sandwich

Many youth who exhibit maladaptive behavior have poor problem-solving skills. In fact, the primary reason why children and adolescents end up in a rehabilitation program is that they have poor problem-solving skills.

The why sandwich is a problem-solving technique. It is a simple technique that can be used at any time. There are three steps in the why sandwich, all of which are also questions.

- The first step involves a 'what' question: *"What is the problem?"*
- The second step involves a 'why' question: *"Why is this a problem?"*
- The final step involves another 'what' question: *"What will I do about the problem?"*

A 'why' question is sandwiched between two 'what' questions, hence the name 'why sandwich.'

What: What is the Problem?

In this step of the problem-solving process, you must identify the problem. Most problems remain unsolved because the person does not understand the problem. The first step in problem-solving is to define the problem in detail in order to have a good understanding of the problem. You can use the following questions to begin identifying your problem:

What is the problem?	*Where did it happen?"*
Who is involved?	*How many times has it happened?*
When did it happen?	*How did it start?*
How did it happen?	*Who knows about the problem?*

Why: Why is this a Problem?

The next step in problem-solving is to understand why the so-called problem is a problem. If you understand why it is a problem, you can understand its seriousness. When you understand why something is a problem, you often understand why you must change the problem. At the same time, when you understand your problem, you can identify your motivation for changing the problem. Ask the following questions to begin understanding why a problem is indeed a problem:

Why is this a problem?   *Are other people hurt?*

Is it part of a pattern?   *Why do others think it is a problem?*

What: What Will I Do About the Problem?

The final 'what' question involves planning action for problem-solving. Once you have identified your problem and understand why it is problem, you need to do something about it. Ask yourself the following questions in order to devise with a plan of action for eliminating your problem. Once you have a plan, take action.

What can I do?   *How can I prevent the problem in the future?*

Can anyone help me?   *What have other people done in a similar situation?*

The Why Sandwich Worksheet

If you use the why sandwich to help youth, you have to know how the why sandwich works. The best way to figure out how the why sandwich works is to practice it on one of your problems.

In the space below, use the why sandwich to solve one of your problems. Since this is the first time you have used the why sandwich, think of a small problem to work on with the why sandwich. Do not pick a large or embarrassing problem. Remember, you are doing this in public and could be called upon to discuss your response. It would not be wise to pick a problem that would embarrass you, such as marital, sexual, or substance-abuse problems.

Above all, choose a problem that you would not mind discussing with the class. For example, in other classes, people have completed why sandwiches for exceeding the speed limit, smoking cigarettes, cussing, being late, procrastinating, working too much, having a dirty house, cleaning too much, and getting the last word in during an argument.

What is the problem? *(Answer who, what, when, where, how, how long, and how often.)*

Why is it a problem? *(Why don't you like it? How does it affect others? Is it part of an overall pattern?)*

What are you going to do about it? *(How are you going to do things differently? What is your goal? How will you reach your goal? Can anyone help you to reach your goal?)*

Role-Playing: Leading and Teaching

Pair up with another trainee. One of you will play the youth, while the other will play the staff member. Each scenario below should last from 1 to 2 minutes. When you are finished, switch roles.

Scenarios

1. It is quiet in the dorm. Most of the youth are out of the dorm, and the few youth in the dorm are working on assignments in their rooms. One youth asks to speak with you and comes to your desk. Only you and the youth are near the desk, so no one else can hear your conversation. The youth tells you that he or she has been thinking about things that the father did to him or her. The youth says that the father did nasty things. After talking briefly, he or she tells you that the father sexually abused him or her, starts to cry, and asks you what you think he or she should do. (*Role-play guideline*: The youth trusts you and really needs to talk to somebody about the abuse.)

2. A youth comes to talk to you in private. The youth says that he or she is tired of screwing up and complains that, though trying to do well, he or she just keeps messing up. The youth asks for advice about how to get through a day without messing up. (*Role-play guideline*: The youth is sincere.)

3. A youth complains about just not being able to get along with his or her roommate. You decide to help the youth by completing a why sandwich. In a role-play activity, complete a why sandwich with the youth.

4. A youth tells you that he or she had an upsetting call from home. He or she has learned his or her little brother is in juvenile detention and that the mother cannot make rent. The youth tells you that he or she feels like exploding. You must help the youth to recognize, label, and deal with these emotions.

Checking

Checking is a structured confrontation between two youths. A youth checks a peer when the youth observes his or her peer violating rules or engaging in conduct disordered youth behavior.

Checking is a technique that mobilizes peer pressure in a prosocial manner. Checking is powerful because it can happen anytime, anywhere, and even when staff members are not around.

Since checking is a form of confrontation, it is potentially explosive. Youths must therefore be taught the proper way to check.

How to Check:

1. Teach the youth how to discriminate between positive behavior (e.g., giving or receiving help) and negative behavior (e.g., conduct disordered youth behavior).
2. Teach the youth to expect positive behavior to be rewarded and negative behavior confronted.
3. Explain to youth that one way to give help is to confront the negative behavior of peers.
4. Provide training and examples of how to check, such as what follows:

Situation: *Tony is hitting a weaker peer. Billy sees the assault.*

Billy: Tony! Check yourself. You know you can't hit or horseplay.

Tony: Screw you. You fool. Don't tell me what to do!

Billy: Check yourself. You are not receiving help.

Tony: I'll help you by hitting you!

Billy: You can check yourself or we can go to a huddle-up. It's your choice.

Tony: Okay, okay.

Potential Pitfalls

1. **Burn games:** A youth or group of youths might target a peer to abuse. These youths could check the targeted peers for minor infractions or no infractions at all. The youth receiving the inappropriate checks could become angry and act out and, in turn, suffer the consequences. If this occurs, the targeted peer has been "burned" by his peers.

2. **Mr. Goodguy/Ms. Goodgal:** Some youth use checking to appear to be prosocial. They will check other youths when staff is around. When staff is not around, these youths act out. The youth uses checks in front of staff to create a false front that hides his or her delinquency.

3. **Lack of support:** Though a youth could check appropriately, conduct disordered youth peers might not respond. Any nonresponsive conduct disordered youth peer is testing the limits not of the peers but of the staff. If staff members do not support a peer who is checking appropriately, it undermines program integrity. By contrast, if staff do support a positive youth, it decreases the likelihood that the conduct disordered youth will act out. Remember that preventing acting out is what behavior management is all about.

Youth who check should know that it is not their job to stop any negative behavior but only to check the behavior. If the behavior does not stop, they can request a huddle-up.

Behavior Groups

The behavior group is a group conducted by direct care or security staff for the purpose of letting youth talk about how things are going on the dorm. If there are problems, the youth can solve problems in daily living in the behavior group. It is important to understand what a behavior group is *not*:

- The behavior group is *not* a therapy or rehabilitation group. To do therapy, you have to focus on what the youth did prior to coming to the program. Instead, the behavior group deals with problems that arise in the dorm or facility. Its goal is to prevent acting out.
- The behavior group is *not* individual therapy. In individual therapy, the staff person talks to one youth. In a large group, the staff gets all the youth involved and youth talk to each other.

There are four steps to conducting a behavior group. Each of these steps is explained in detail below.

Elect a peer leader	<ul><li>The peer leader from the previous group session nominates two peers, who stand to explain why he or she would be a good group leader.</li><li>After all group members vote, the youth who receives the majority of votes is elected peer leader for the day.</li><li>The peer leader uses a notebook to log layouts</li></ul>
Layout	<ul><li>Each group member completes a layout.</li><li>Other group members listen to their peers' layouts and afterward confront the peer if there are any inaccuracies.</li></ul>
Problem Solving	<ul><li>The peer leader determines which youth gets to present his or her topic.</li><li>Prioritize topics accordingly: crises and severe problems, chronic problems, and personal agendas.</li></ul>

	• **Why Sandwich** – use the why sandwich to solve problems during the behavior group.
Conclusion	• The staff member gets the last word by praising and labeling.
	• **Praise:** The staff member should catch and praise youth behaving correctly.
	• **Labeling behavior:** The staff member should identify and devalue conduct disordered youth behavior.

If you are doing most of the talking during a behavior group, you are doing something wrong. The youths should be doing most of the talking.

You must mobilize peer pressure by requiring that youths do one of two things: give or receive help. Remember to use peer influence; it is more powerful than any words you speak. You should not be part of the discussion but instead guide it.

Behavior Group Layout

My name is _____

Since the last behavior group, I have had the following successes: _____

_____

Since the last behavior group, I have caused the following problems: _____

_____

My behavior problem that I would like to work on during this behavior group is _____

_____

Behavior Management Group Log

Dorm: _____ Date: _____ Time: _____

Staff Leader: _____ Peer Leader: _____

Youth	Topic	Assignment

Behavior Group Rules

The following is a list of rules that should be adhered to during a behavior group session. All youths should be taught these rules during orientation. On occasion, it might be wise to have youths recite these rules during a behavior group. It should be noted that some staff members require the peer leader to recite the group rules in every group session prior to starting layouts.

- Sit correctly with both feet on the floor, hands in your lap, and all legs of the chair on the floor.
- Raise your hand and be recognized before speaking.
- When voting for a peer leader, raise your hand above your ear.
- Do not speak when someone else has the floor.
- When presenting your layout, make eye contact.
- When giving or receiving feedback, make eye contact.
- There are only two things you can do in group: give or receive help. You give help by being supportive or confronting acting out. You receive help by accepting feedback or learning by watching a peer receive feedback.
- Have your successes, behavior problems, and topics in mind before arriving to group. You need to go through layouts quickly.
- If you are given an assignment in one group session, have it ready by the next session.
- If you get kicked out of group, expect to have to do work to get back into group. There are always more consequences to getting kicked out of group than staying in it.

Be aware that group rules are intended to create a safe, orderly group atmosphere. Some youth will misuse group rules by playing burn games, testing limits, or distracting.

Helpful Hints for Conducting a Behavior Group

General Hints

- Be direct. Control the group.

- Never lose control of the group.

- Dismiss the whole group if necessary.

- There should be more consequences for a youth to be dismissed from group than to stay in it. That is, a youth should have to compensate for being kicked out of group.

- If the whole group is kicked out, the whole group should receive consequences.

- Confront sooner, not later. Never lose control of the group.

- Expel sooner rather than later. Never lose control of the group.

- Fill the room with your presence. Youth must know that it is your group, but you must control the group through the peer leader.

- Set limits on acting out and praise good behavior.

- Make comments and confront quickly. Then turn managing the group over to the peer leader.

- Be skeptical. If you think there is more to a youth's story, there probably is. Be skeptical and probe.

- You can talk about a youth after he or she is kicked out of group. Do not put down the youth kicked out of group. Prepare the group to be positive and work with that youth in the future.

- Deal directly with signs of a delinquent environment (e.g., gang signs or support of negative values). Confront and give consequences to youth who show support for a delinquent environment.

- Deal with youth who control the group in a negative way.

- If you start a confrontation, finish it. Nothing will undermine your power more quickly than not finishing a confrontation. Youth will think that you are weak. Since youth will not expect to finish confrontations in the future, they will resist your confrontations expecting that it is only matter of time before you run out of gas again.

Electing a Peer Leader

- The best way to control the group is by using the peer leader.
- This is the only time a youth has to stand. The speech that the youth gives should be positive.
- A youth can say they do not want to be group leader, but he or she must still give a speech.
- Tie votes are broken by allowing the nominees to give more information and then by taking another vote.
- Staff members should never break a tie vote.

Layouts

- Complete layouts quickly. Spend no more than 1 to 2 minutes per layout.
- The topics should be specific.

Problem-solving

- Use the why sandwich.
- Emphasize giving and receiving help.
- Do not let unproductive problem-solving continue. If youth are working hard to help a peer and the peer is rejecting the help, confront that youth about not receiving help.

Conclusion

- Praise youth who do well. Be specific. Tell them what they did and praise each youth as a person.
- Label acting out behavior and warn that it will lead a person to ruin.

Helpful Phrases

- *"What thinking error are you using?"*
- *"Group, what do you think?"*
- *"Group leader, would you find out what he or she is doing right now?"*
- *"Is that giving or receiving help?"*

Thinking Leads to Emotions and Behavior

Your thoughts determine how you feel. Your thoughts and feelings together determine how you act.

Most people believe that an event leads to an emotion (i.e., event → emotion). This is not true. You can give yourself a test right now. Suppose there is a political election and a Republican gets elected. How do you think the all of the Republicans will feel? How will the Democrats feel? If you said that the Republicans and Democrats would feel differently, you just proved the point. Events do not cause emotions; emotions are caused by what people think about events.

Let's extend this situation a little farther. Suppose the Republicans were happy with the election results. How do you think they will act? Now, suppose that the Democrats are unhappy with the results. How do you think they will act? Understand that thinking and feeling determines action. Study the chart above, and follow the arrows.

Can you use this information to help you do your job better? Remember that your job is to manage behavior. This information shows you that if you really want to get control over a youth's behavior, you have to get control over the way they are thinking because thinking leads to emotions and behavior. Better still is teaching the youths to control their own thinking.

Two important things to focus on in order to help youth control their thinking are thinking errors and self-control techniques. You will be learning about thinking errors and self-control techniques in the next two lessons.

Thinking Errors

Thinking precedes action. Before anyone can perform a particular act, he or she must think about doing that act. The way in which someone thinks determines how he or she will act. People who think depressed thoughts will act depressed, while people who think happy thoughts will act happy. By the same token, people who think delinquent thoughts will act like a delinquent.

The specific ways in which a conduct disordered youth thinks differ from the ways in which citizens think. These specific thinking patterns are known as *thinking errors*. Conduct disordered youth thinking errors lead to acting out. Some of the more common thinking errors used by conduct disordered youths are listed below.

Power play: I try to dominate, manipulate, and control others. I know the right way to do things, but I prefer to do things *my way*. I view every situation as a win or a loss, and I will do anything, even wrong or illegal things, to make sure that I win.

Closed channel: I am close-minded. My communication is the opposite of open communication, and I do not reveal my true thoughts and feelings. I do not accept feedback from others.

Secretiveness: I use secrets to control others, to make myself feel powerful, and to continue being delinquent. I try to develop secret relationships with others who I think will help me act out. I develop secret relationships with people who I plan to manipulate or abuse. I also use secrets in treatment to avoid letting other people know me.

Entitlement: I think the world owes me. I feel superior to others, even though I have done nothing to earn that feeling. I want others to treat me as though I were special and, if they refuse, I get mad, and I get even.

Keeping score: I keep track of the times when a particular person has confronted me, argues with me, or does me wrong. When I think that the other person is in a position of weakness, I attack that person. I try to hurt them in order to even the score.

Selfishness: I do not show concern or sympathy for others. I fail to consider the rights and feelings of others. I do what I want to do, both when I want to do it, and regardless of whom I disappoint or hurt.

Hop Over: I do not answer questions when I know the answer will be unpleasant. I evade, or hop over, the question by answering a different question or changing the subject. I try to change the subject or redefine a problem so that I do not have to talk about things I do not want to.

Poor me: I try to look like I am hurt or like everyone is picking on me. I get others to give me love and support so that I will not have to be responsible. I will use this thinking to get people in authority to switch from holding me accountable to becoming my rescuer.

Victim's Stance: I try to replace the real victim by convincing others that I was more hurt than the victim.

Pet me: I do things just to get others to praise me. My heart is not in what I am doing. I am just trying to get others to tell me, "Good job" or "That a boy."

Mr. Goodguy / Ms. Goodgal: I wear a mask or a false front. I give the right answer as well as do or say the right thing, even though that is not how I truly think and feel. On the outside, I appear to be a good citizen but underneath this mask is a juvenile delinquent.

Confusion: I look confused though I know what is going on. I try to convince others to believe that I do not know what to do or what is expected of me. I typically use confusion as a way to avoid responsibility or as an excuse for not doing what I was supposed to do.

Helplessness: I present myself as incapable and unable to do what I am asked. I think if I look helpless, people do not expect much of me, so I will not be held accountable.

Justifying: I make excuses or explanations for my inappropriate behavior. I try to make something wrong appear as if it were not wrong.

Blaming: I blame someone or something for causing me to act as I do. I blame others so I can avoid responsibility for my actions.

Minimizing: I try to make wrong behavior appear insignificant. Sometimes I compare my wrong behavior to worse behavior in order to seem good by comparison.

Mindreading: I assume that I know the thoughts, motives, and intentions of other people. I don't bother to ask other people what they think or what is important to them.

Anger: I feel angry in most situations and get angry easily. My anger quickly becomes intense and spreads. I use tantrums, outrage, and aggression to express anger. When I am angry, I do not think in a normal, rational way. My anger can leads to acting out. I use anger sometimes to shift the focus off a problem. I also use anger to seek revenge. Sometimes I get angry or pretend that I am angry so I can justify hurting someone.

Super-Optimism: I believe I am such a slick, criminal person that no one will catch me or become wise to my criminal tricks and plans. I am aware that if I do wrong and get caught, I will get punished. However, I never think I will get caught, and that if I do, I will be able to talk my way out of it.

Ownership: I view other people as possessions and act as if I have total control over other people. I ignore the other person's feelings and needs and abuse power in the relationship.

Making Fools Of: I exaggerate the mistakes and weaknesses of others in order to put them down so that I can feel superior. If I do this in public, I am trying to raise my status by tearing down another person. Sometimes I just do this in my mind, so I can disrespect someone privately.

Can't Wait: I am impulsive. I do not wait for the proper time to do things. I cannot delay my desires. I do what I want when I want, even if it is not an appropriate time.

Jail House Lawyer: I use legalistic arguments to create a cloud of words in order to confuse and distract others from what is really relevant. I skillfully focus on rules or morals and hide behind them so that others cannot force me to be responsible. I especially like to ignore the spirit of a law or rule by using a literal interpretation in order to mislead others. I divert attention from real issues by focusing on irrelevant, petty details.

Zero State: I feel worthless. I feel like I'm a nothing. I believe that things will never change and that I will always be a zero. I may engage in illegal or dangerous activities so that I can prove to others or myself that I am not a zero.

Uniqueness: I feel that I am different…and better than others. Even if my crime is similar, I have ways of proving that I am different and better. I think that because I am different, what applies to others does not apply to me. This feeling is especially true when it comes to rules, laws, and consequences. I believe that if people would just realize how different I was, they would realize that rules or consequences do not apply to me.

Criminal pride: I take pride in acting out. My self-esteem is based on my acting out and delinquent accomplishments, e.g., breaking rule or breaking the law. I take pride in getting away with acting out.

Criminal Outlets

The word "criminal" and "delinquent" are used rarely in the Limit & Lead Program. In fact, about the only time we use these words is when using a technique known as over correction.

The therapy technique of over correction is labeling a thought or behavior in a very negative way. The label has to be so negative that the person doesn't want that label applied to him or her.

In the Limit & Lead workbook that youths use to learn to control their acting out, over correction is used to label undesirable behaviors. We call these behaviors criminal outlets.

A criminal outlet is any behavior based on thinking errors. In this sense, thinking errors always lead to criminal outlets. There are two types of criminal outlets: criminal precursors and crime.

Criminal Precursors

Some criminal outlets are not illegal. They are morally or socially wrong and can lead to crime. Since moral and social violations can lead to crime, these inappropriate behaviors are called *criminal precursors*.

Lying	*Cheating*	*Selfishness*	*Insulting*
Gossiping	*Cursing*	*Self-indulgence*	*Limit testing*
Jealously	*False pride*	*Greed*	*Envy*
Disorderliness	*Hostility*	*Craving*	*Deception/secretiveness*

The criminal precursors listed above are not actual crimes. For example, there are no state laws against greed or envy. However, if a youth lets these values guide his or her behavior, it is only a matter of time before he or she commits a crime.

The goal of the Limit & Lead Program is **No More Victims**. Therefore, it is important for youths to recognize and stop their criminal precursors. If a youth can recognize and stop all criminal precursors, he or she will have **No More Victims.**

Crime

A crime is acting out that breaks the law; it is a violation of the penal code. The major categories of crimes are listed below.

Theft	*Robbery*	*Perjury*	*Assault*
Murder	*Resisting arrest*	*Sex offenses*	*Use of a weapon*
Fraud	*Escaping/absconding*	*Kidnapping*	*Arson*
Treason	*Vandalism*	*Driving violations*	*Family violence*
Drug-related crimes	*Trespassing*	*Alcohol-related crimes*	*Curfew violations*

Youth in the Limit & Lead Program are expected to know and monitor their urges for criminal outlets. All staff members should also know these criminal outlets so that they can confront youth who use criminal precursors or commit crimes.

The Offense Cycle and Stair Steps

If the behavior management program operates effectively, the youth in the program will be able to make progress in rehabilitation activities such as anger management, sex offender treatment, and substance abuse treatment.

Security staff and direct care staff can do more than just provide a safe environment for youths to make progress in rehabilitation activities. Direct care and security staff can learn the basics of the rehabilitation program and then help the youths work on rehabilitation.

The most basic thing a youth learns to do in rehabilitation activities is to control their offense cycle. Let's break down the term "offense cycle." A cycle is a pattern that happens repeatedly. An offense is a crime. So, an offense cycle is a youth's repeated pattern of behavior that ends with the youth committing an offense.

Below are the steps of the offense cycle. This offense cycle works for any kind of criminal act, e.g., theft, assault, robbery, sexual assault, criminal mischief, DWI, trespassing, and vandalism. Definitions for each step of the offense cycle are presented beneath the model.

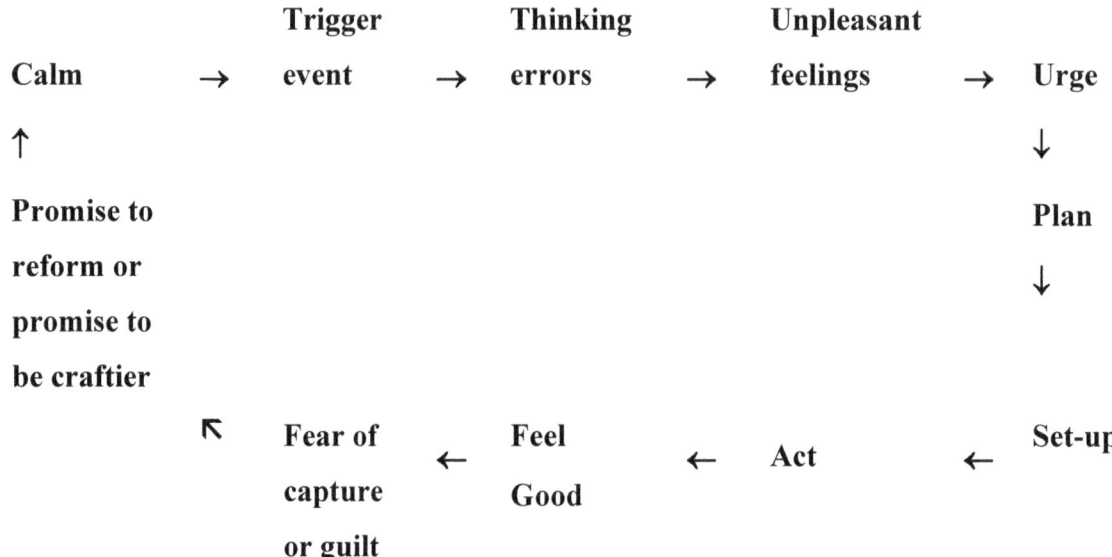

Trigger event: A trigger event is any stressful event; any kind of stress could trigger the offense cycle. Common triggers include an argument, a relationship problem, a problem at school, or a disappointment. On the surface, a trigger looks completely unrelated to criminal behavior.

Thinking error: The youth uses thinking errors while thinking about the trigger event. The youth will probably use more than one thinking error.

Unpleasant feelings: The ways that the youth thinks about the trigger event creates unpleasant feelings (i.e., sadness, anger, or fear). For example, the trigger event might be an argument with his or her father. The youth might use the thinking error of *keeping score*, such as, "Dad always treats me like a kid. He does it all the time." This type of thinking leads to the unpleasant feeling of anger.

Urge: Unpleasant feelings don't feel good, so the youth starts thinking about different ways to make himself or herself feel better. A lot of different fantasies run through the youth's mind. A fantasy is both a mental picture and the feeling created by that picture. For example, the youth can picture him or herself engaging in vandalism at school. The youth gets a happy and excited feeling while fantasizing about the different ways he or she can damage school property.

Plan: Planning is nothing more than devising a way to turn the criminal fantasy into a reality. Some plans are simple (e.g., wait until no one is looking), while others are complicated and tricky.

Set-up: The set-up is anything that the youth does to make sure that he or she can commit the crime and get away with it. Sometimes this step is called *manipulation*. For example, if a youth wants to assault a rival, he or she might manipulate the rival into meeting at an isolated location.

Act: The act is a criminal act but it is much more than a crime. It is the way that the youth chose to make himself or herself feel better in response to the trigger. The act is also the result of planning and set-up. Crimes don't just happen and they have meaning to the youth.

Feel Good: The youth feels good right after the crime. The youth can make his or her satisfaction last longer by reliving or rehashing the crime to other conduct disordered youth.

Guilt or fear of capture: After the initial satisfaction disappears, the youth begins having doubts about having committed the crime. For the first time, he or she thinks that it is possible to get caught and punished, which can provoke his or her fear.

Promise: The youth fools him or herself into thinking that he or she will not get caught by promising to reform. Sometimes the offender even makes this promise to the victim. Other offenders promise to be a craftier, more professional offender.

The offense cycle is the signature way that youth commit crimes. In the terminology of law enforcement, any offense cycle is a youth's *modus operandi*, or the habitual way that he or she commits crimes.

It can be depressing to consider that a youth has committed enough crimes that they actually have a 'signature way' of committing crimes. Though depressing, the offense cycle also has advantages. Since the youth learned his or her offense cycle, then he or she can also unlearn the cycle. In fact, several of the assignments that youth work on in treatment sessions are designed to help each youth to unlearn his or her offense cycle, so they can have **No More Victims.**

Stair Steps

The offense cycle is pretty long and has many steps. There is actually a simpler from of the offense cycle that direct care and security staff may want to use. This simpler version of the offense cycle is known as the *stair steps*. The stair steps are composed of the first seven steps of the offense cycle.

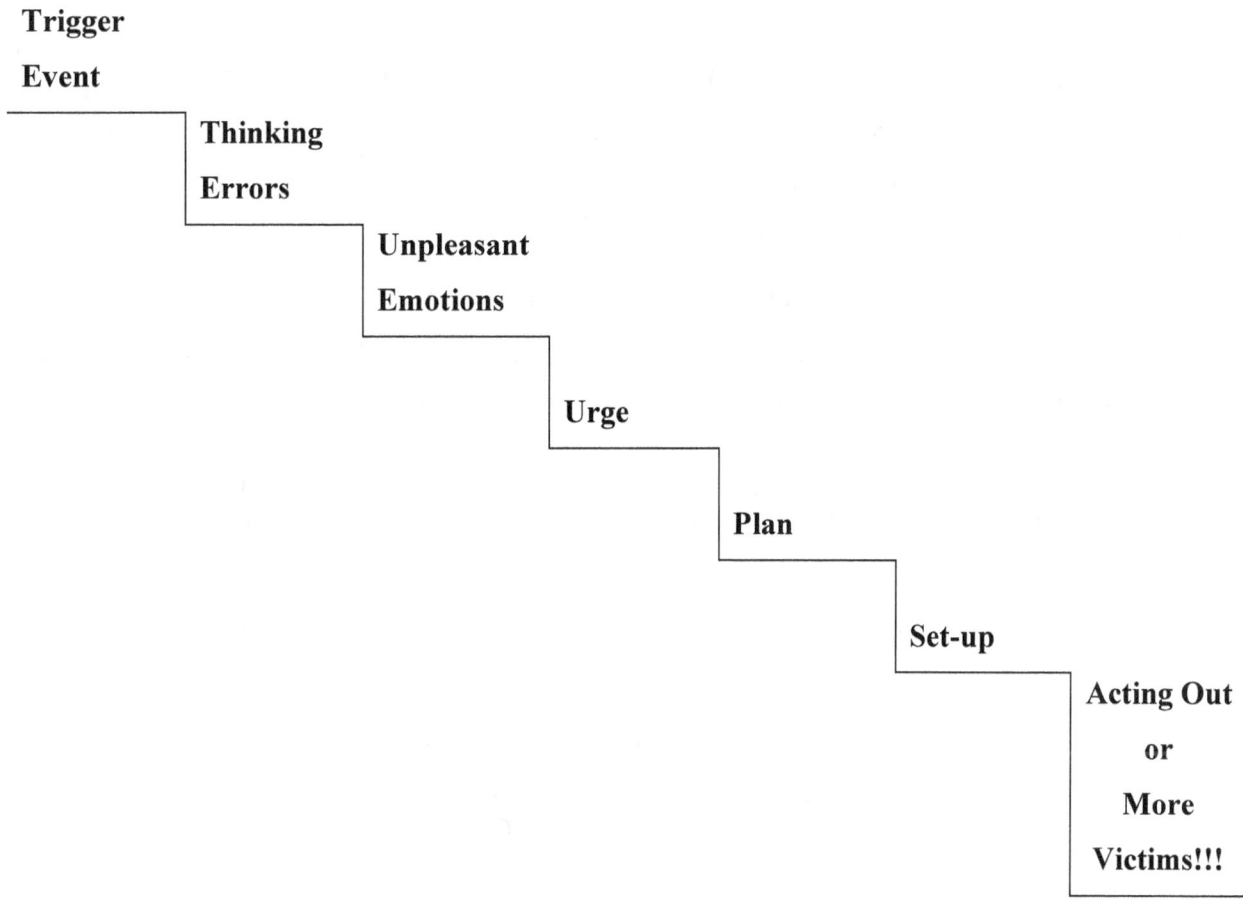

As a direct care staff or security staff, you will not be responsible for approving rehabilitation assignments completed by youth. However, youth may need your help working on these assignments, so you should know and understand the offense cycle.

If you develop a really good understanding of the offense cycle, you can use this concept when supervising youth. For example, you can confront a youth for acting out behavior and you can let him or her know that the acting out behavior is part of their patter, i.e., it is an offense cycle. You and the youth can break down the behavior and identify the different steps in the offense cycle. Once you have identified the steps, the youth can work on ways to recognize and stop his or her offense cycle. If you can do this, you can help the youth reach the goal of **No More Victims**.

ACE: Self-Control Techniques

Being able to recognize thinking errors, criminal outlets, and the offense cycle is not enough to reach the goal of **No More Victims**. The youth must also learn how to control these things by using different coping techniques.

In the Limit & Lead Program, coping techniques are referred to as ACE. ACE is an acronym for all possible coping techniques; ACE stands for *avoid*, *cope*, and *escape*. For any problem that a youth faces, he or she can cope by using *avoid, cope or escape.*

Avoid: To prevent crime, the youth should avoid situations, places, and people that increase the youth's likelihood of acting out. The youth must be smart enough to know the people, places, and situations that pose risks for him or her, as well as strong enough to stay away.

Cope: All coping techniques are mental techniques used to deal with criminal urges, criminal fantasies, thinking errors, and unpleasant emotions. Some coping techniques a youth could use are as follows:

- **Tunnel vision:** This technique primarily involves redirecting attention. The youth does not pay attention to the person or situation causing the unwanted thoughts but instead redirects his or her attention to responsible thoughts and actions. This technique derives its name from its emphasis on narrowing one's attention, similar to how looking down a tunnel narrows one's vision. For example, if a youth sitting at a table in the dorm sees a peer trying to aggravate him, he or she will look away, stare at his or her work, and avoid looking at the peer.

- **Thought broadcasting:** The youth who uses this technique imagines that his or her thoughts are being broadcast over a loudspeaker system. The youth is taught to imagine that, as his or her thoughts are being broadcast, people look and respond to what they hear being broadcast. The youth decides to stop thinking about acting out because everyone is staring and becoming angry.

- **Reality check:** When a youth performs a reality check, he or she asks questions such as, "How realistic is it that I could actually do what I am thinking?" "What kind of trouble could I get into if I actually tried to do what I am thinking?" and "Is this the behavior of a citizen or a conduct disordered youth? Am I giving or receiving help by doing this?"

- **Reversal:** The youth who uses reversal mentally turns the tables on him or herself. For example, if a youth has a thought of assaulting someone, he or she is told to imagine that a person who he or she does not like is having the same thought toward him or her. The youth is taught to use the unpleasant emotions caused by this possibility to steer him or herself away from thinking this way.

- **The Golden Rule:** "Do unto others as you would have them do unto you"; this is the Golden Rule. Youth are taught that, when they start down the path to acting out, they should stop and use the Golden Rule to get off that path.

Escape: Sometimes a youth may unexpectedly find him or herself in a high-risk situation. For example, a youth may inadvertently come into contact with a person, place, or situation that he or she knows could easily lead to acting out. The youth must be strong and smart enough to leave that situation.

The ACE self-control techniques are designed to help youth change their thinking. If your goal is to use behavior management techniques to prevent negative behavior, you must essentially work on the youth's thinking.

Huddle-Ups

A huddle-up is a behavior management group called by the staff in order to interrupt disruptive youth(s). Though the huddle-up is only one technique that can be used to manage disruptive youth but it is a very powerful technique since it takes advantage of peer pressure.

Even though the huddle-up is a very powerful behavior management intervention, there will be times when you don't want to use the huddle-up, e.g., you do not know the youths, you know the youths to be negative, or youth are intimidated by the negative youth.

Situations Calling for a Huddle-Up:

- Verbal aggression
- Threat of overt aggression
- Flagrant violations of the rights of others
- Failing to respond to staff confrontation
- Serious challenges to staff authority which might lead to physical confrontation

Before Initiating a Huddle-Up:

- Only staff may initiate a huddle-up, though youth can request a huddle-up.
- Staff only initiate a huddle-up when they are certain that the outcome will be positive.
- Staff should consider all alternatives before initiating a huddle-up.
- Staff should consider the location of the huddle-up.
- Staff should consider the time of the huddle-up.

Directions for Organizing a Huddle-Up:

1. **Beginning:** A staff member calls for a huddle-up and identifies the problem and the youth with the problem. The staff member appoints a youth to lead the discussion.
2. **Problem-solving:** The youth's peers begin to help the disruptive youth, during which time it may be wise to use the vegetarian why sandwich (i.e., without the 'why' question). This step should generate alternatives to the disruptive behavior.

3. **Agreement:** The disruptive youth agrees to cease the disruptive behavior and commit to an alternative behavior.

4. **Conclusion:** The staff member concludes the huddle-up.

The huddle-up is only one technique used to interrupt disruptive behavior. However, whenever possible, staff should use the huddle-up since it is such a powerful way to manage the environment.

Anatomy of a Crisis

A crisis is any situation in which a youth or group of youth becomes increasingly out of control. In crisis situations, staff will have to step in and establish control.

If you want to control a crisis, you should use what you learned about offense cycles. When you studied the offense cycle, you learned that a crime doesn't just happen. Something leads up to an offense. The same is true for a crisis. A crisis doesn't just happen. Something always leads up to a crisis. Below is an outline of how a crisis develops.

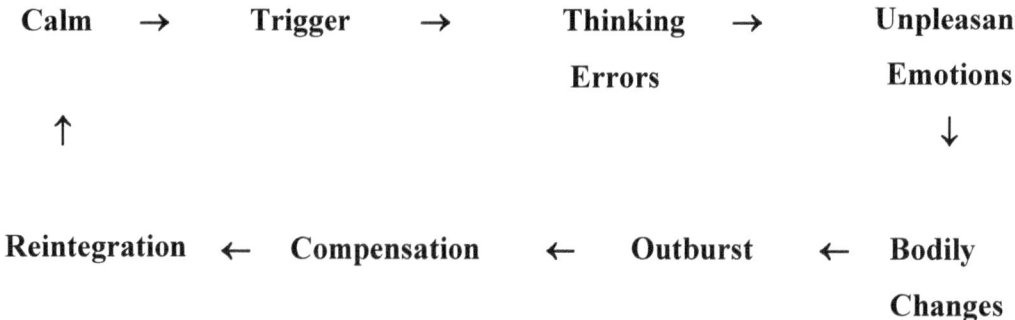

Trigger: The most common trigger to a crisis is stress. Stress is part of life. For youth in the program, there is *always* a trigger for a crisis because there is always stress. These youth typically have poor coping skills and consequently do not effectively manage their stress. Expect these youth to become frustrated in response to stress. Frustration is not static, and it invariably gives way to aggression.

Thinking errors: When a youth thinks about stress, he or she will use thinking errors. Thinking errors only worsen situations and certainly do nothing to eliminate stress.

Unpleasant emotions: Thinking errors always lead to unpleasant emotions, i.e., sadness, fear, and anger. These feelings can actually increase the stress that a youth feels.

Bodily changes: Before a youth becomes aggressive or violent, his or her body changes. Blood begins to flow to the muscles and heart rate and respiration increase. A youth might feel weak in the knees or have butterflies in the stomach. Regardless of how it feels, the body feels different as the youth builds up to an outburst.

Outburst: The outburst is what people readily identify as a crisis. An outburst occurs when a youth makes a verbal or physical outburst.

Compensation: After an outburst, the youth undergoes a period during which he or she must pull it together and compensate. An outburst can disorient the youth, and it takes some time before he or she can return to feeling like him or herself.

Reintegration: The youth who has made an outburst has alienated him or herself from positive peers and staff members. The youth must somehow work his or her way back into the mainstream of the program.

A crisis is always a process. If the process goes uninterrupted, it will result in an outburst. However, since something always leads up to a crisis, you can intervene and stop a crisis before it occurs. You can also act after an outburst in order to ensure that other crises do not occur.

Crisis Intervention

Crisis intervention consists of anything you do to stop an outburst. Since a crisis is a process that unfolds over time, you have many different points in time when you could intervene.

The best time to intervene is before a crisis occurs. When you notice a particular youth escalating or 'pumping up' for an outburst, it is time to intervene. You should also use the time after an outburst to prevent future outbursts. Here, as in other procedures, prevention is key.

Shown in the table below are all of the different points in the crisis process at which you can intervene. Notice how the intervention changes according to each step in the process.

Crisis Process Step	Detection	Intervention
Trigger	The youth • appears frustrated. • has difficulty expressing him or herself. • may start to make a request and then give up. • has vague complaints. • does not appear to be taking good care of him or herself	Hold a one-on-one discussion in which you help the youth identify his or her needs and frustrations. This is a good time to use the why sandwich.

Thinking errors	The youth • appears to be pumping up for a fight • uses aggressive thinking errors, such as "It's not fair" and putting down others.	Isolate the youth away from the others. Get the youth to focus on his or her thinking. If possible, get the youth to write down and identify aggressive thinking errors and help the youth to replace conduct disordered youth thinking with citizen thinking.
Unpleasant emotions	• The youth feels unpleasant emotions (e.g., anger, fear, and sadness).	Help the youth to recognize and express the emotion. Sometimes it is helpful to get the youth to write in a journal.
Bodily Changes	• Clenched fist • Clinched jaw • Pacing • Mad-dogging • Tunnel vision • Muscular tension	Pull the youth aside. Get the youth to start breathing deeply. Let the youth engage in physical exercise but *not* punching of any kind (e.g., upon pillows and mattresses)
Outburst	• Verbal or physical aggression	Restrain or place the youth in security.
Compensation	• The technical term for this stage is *regression*, during which the youth is disoriented, cannot think straight, and may be or become emotionally and physically exhausted.	Do not talk much or overly process the incident. Let the youth know you are in charge, that they are safe, and that you will keep everyone else safe, too.

Reintegration	• The youth is calm. There are no aggressive thinking errors or somatic changes.	The youth could write a clarification letter to those harmed. The youth should discuss the outburst in a behavior group and could additionally meet with positive peers outside of behavior group to hear peer expectations.

De-escalating a Crisis

If you have to de-escalate an outburst, the youth has arrived at the step of the crisis process at which somatic changes become evident. Otherwise, the youth may already be at the stage of making an outburst (i.e., verbal or physical aggression).

If the youth is only using verbal aggression, you can still try to de-escalate the outburst. However, if the youth is using physical aggression and he or she appears to be a threat to him or herself or others, physical restraint is the correct response.

Keep some basic guidelines in mind when conducting de-escalation. For example, de-escalation is most effective when you address the crisis on several levels at the same time. The acronym LEAD is a good way to de-escalate a crisis. To use LEAD, take the following steps in this order:

L - Limit the environment. Take away the youth's audience and potential victims. You can do this by removing the disruptive youth from the area. If this youth is too volatile, then you can remove the other youth. Be careful to avoid making quick or aggressive gestures. Maintain an appropriate social distance, and do not crowd or touch the disruptive youth.

E - Empathize with the disruptive youth's situation and feelings. Remember that most crises begin with a communication breakdown. Express your empathy for how this youth may feel. Deal with his or her interests, needs, and feelings.

A - Alternatives should be offered. In fact, you should bombard the disruptive youth with alternatives. Your goal is to offer so many alternatives that the youth must stop and think. Once you the youth is thinking about the alternatives, he or she is not using aggressive thinking. If the youth abandons aggressive thinking and instead focuses on the various alternatives offered, his or her somatic symptoms will gradually decrease. In a sense, it is not really important what you get the youth to think about as long as you offer enough alternative behaviors for the situation.

D - Decisions are made by the youth to use an appropriate alternative. The youth must commit to an alternative as well as agree to meet his or her needs in an appropriate manner.

The most important thing that you can do during a crisis intervention is to empathize. At the same time, the most important thing that you can get the disruptive youth to do is consider alternatives. Remember that when a youth is considering alternatives, he or she is not merely considering alternatives but refocusing his or her thoughts and abandoning aggressive thinking.

Empathize + Distract = De-escalation

The Anatomy of a Delinquent Game

A delinquent game is a planned manipulation of the staff. Though there are many games that conduct disordered youths try to play with staff, all of them have several things in common:

1. The game is designed to benefit the youth.
2. The game is designed to manipulate and harm the staff.
3. All delinquent games follow the same process.

A delinquent game is designed to let the youth gain power and control. If you were to ask a conduct disordered youth, he or she would tell you that the best delinquent games give him or her power and control over a victim. Of course, the victim in a delinquent game is always **YOU**, the staff member.

Delinquent games do not materialize out of thin air. The youth must do certain things in order to play a delinquent game. An outline for the delinquent game is presented below.

Observe Staff	→	Select a victim	→	Set-up	→	Seemingly Unimportant Event
↑						↓
Compensating ←		Turning the tables ←		Waiting ←		Exploitation

Observe Staff: The youth observes all staff all the time. He or she selects victims based upon their tendencies.

Select a victim: Based upon his or her observations, the youth goes through the process of elimination and then selects a staff member that he or she could easily victimize.

Setting-up: Having settled upon a particular staff member to victimize, the youth will try to isolate this staff member from the others (e.g., by ego-boosting). Once the staff member is isolated, the staff member is no longer a staff member. He or she becomes a victim.

A seemingly unimportant event: A seemingly unimportant event is a small thing that the staff person does to treat the youth special. The special treatment might not be an actual rule violation but it is something that the staff wouldn't have done prior to be set-up.

Exploitation: The youth continues to get the staff person to give him or her special treatment. Eventually, the youth manipulates the staff person into violating rules, so the staff can give the youth special treatment.

Waiting: As the youth continues to exploit the staff person, sooner or later the youth's peers and the victim's coworkers will notice that something is wrong. The staff person is asked if there is something going on. Of course, the staff person denies it but knows it is only a matter of time before his or her misconduct is discovered.

Turning the tables: Someone reports the staff's misconduct to the facility administration. When the youth is confronted, the youth turns the tables, i.e., switches from being the one in control to the victim. The youth says he or she wants to come clean and explain how the staff person was the one who was in control of everything. The staff person who the youth exploited is fired from his or her job and may face criminal prosecution.

Compensating: Even when the delinquent game is busted, it is a win-win situation for the youth. The youth got the special treatment while the delinquent game was going on and the youth gets the satisfaction of knowing he or she really hurt the staff person who was exploited. The youth replays the delinquent game over and over in his or her mind as a way to feel happy. As a way to gain status with peers, the youth tells stories to other delinquent youth about how the staff person exploited. Eventually the happy feelings fade and the youth is ready to play a new delinquent game…with a new victim.

How to Avoid Becoming a Victim: Part I

The only way to avoid becoming a victim of a delinquent game is by prevention. As a staff member, if you think that you are involved in a delinquent game, you must take preventative action during the first four steps of the delinquent game.

In this lesson, we will focus on the first two steps of the delinquent game: Observing Staff and Selecting a Victim. The youth's area of interest is shown in the top half of the table below. In the bottom half of the table, write your plan for prevention.

Overcoming the First Step of a Delinquent game: Observing Staff

The youth examines you as you interact with other staff members in order to decide whether you would make a good victim. If you show any of the following, the youth will think you will be an easy victim:	The youth also examines you as you interact with his or her peers in order to decide whether you would make a good victim. If you show any of the following, the youth will find a way to make you his or her victim:
<ul><li>Any extreme tendencies</li><li>Excessive friendliness</li><li>Inexperience</li><li>Dislike for the job</li><li>Sloppy clothing</li><li>Revealing clothing</li><li>Overconfidence</li><li>Low confidence</li><li>Relationships with superiors</li><li>Doubt and/or confusion</li><li>A need for praise</li></ul>	<ul><li>Personal likes</li><li>Personal dislikes</li><li>Family history</li><li>Views on sex</li><li>Views on politics</li><li>Recreational activities</li><li>Social activities</li><li>Emotional status</li><li>Sense of humor</li><li>Career plans</li><li>Criticism of job and/or home</li></ul>

In the space below, list behaviors you have around other staff members that could make you a target for victimization.	In the space below, list behaviors you have around conduct disordered youth that could make you a target for victimization.

Overcoming the Second Step of a Delinquent game: Selecting a Victim

In this step of the delinquent game, the youth tests you in different ways. If you show any weakness, you could become the victim of a delinquent game. The table below shows typical questions and interactions that a youth uses to test you for your suitability as a victim. How would you respond to each question or interaction?

If you have difficulty responding, know that you could always use the following simple response to the youth's tests: "If I responded to your questions [or invitations, etc.], how would that help you to reach your goal of **No More Victims**?"

If you use this response, the youth will likely offer an off-the-wall response, after which you can focus on the off-the-wall response instead of the question he or she posed. This is a quick and effective way to remove yourself from the youth's list of potential victims.

67

Youth's Testing Method	Your Response
• "Are you married?"	•
• "What did the two Hispanic gravediggers say when they went to get a drink?"	•
• "What's your favorite hobby?"	•
• "Do you mind if I do my homework in my room instead of at one of the tables in the dayroom?"	•
• "Do you like women with large breasts or big butts?"	•
• "Do you work another job?"	•
• "Do you have kids?"	•
• "How can you understand me if you don't have kids? Do you have kids?"	•
• "Do you think Nurse Sandra is hot?"	•

How to Avoid Becoming a Victim: Part II

The third and fourth steps of the delinquent game are the set-up and a seemingly unimportant event. In the table below, the youth's area of interest during these two steps is described. As in the previous lesson, you have the opportunity to write your prescription for prevention in the bottom half of the table.

Dealing with the Third Step of a Delinquent game: Setting-Up

The set-up is all about creating a special relationship with you, the staff member who has been selected as a possible victim. If the youth can create a special relationship with you, then you can be isolated from the other staff members. Once you are isolated, it will be easier to manipulate you.

Keep in mind that the set-up is most often achieved by complimenting, blowing smoke, or any kind of ego-boosting. At other times, the youth sets you up by presenting a mirror image to convince you that you both share similar values, experiences, and interests.

Youth's Testing Method	Your Response
• "You are the only staff member I can talk to."	•
• "You are the best person in the dorm."	•
• "You're smarter than the supervisor. Why aren't you the dorm supervisor?"	•
• "You won't believe this. Back home, I have a beagle, just like you."	•

69

• "Can I empty your trash can?"	•
• "Hey, I got some cookies from home. Want some?"	•
• "I know you watched the Green Bay game last night. How'd they do?"	•
• "Man, I like fishing, too. Once I caught a five-pound bass. What's the biggest fish you've ever caught?"	•
• "If they let youth vote on staff person of the month, you'd get my vote."	•

Overcoming the Fourth Step of a Delinquent game: A Seemingly Unimportant Event

If you find yourself in the fourth stage of a delinquent game, you need to seek help from both other staff members and your supervisor. Let them know that you have been targeted as a victim. If you have violated agency policy, report is as soon as possible; it will come out sooner or later, and sooner is always better. Furthermore, self-reporting is always better than being reported by someone else.

In addition to seeking help and self-reporting, you must also re-establish boundaries with the youth who has targeted you. In the space below, describe how you would respond after each having performed each event listed in the left-hand column.

A Seeming Unimportant Event	How Would You Recover from the Seemingly Unimportant Event?
• You let the youth stay up past curfew.	•

• You found a way to get the youth extra commissary.	•
• You gave the youth preferred seating.	•
• You let the youth go first in line.	•
• You let the youth keep minor contraband, such as a pen or staples.	•
• You mailed a letter for the youth.	•
• You brought in clothing for the youth.	•
• You contacted a family member for the youth.	•
• You gave the youth some food from your home.	•

Coping with Delinquent Games: Small Group Discussion

Break into small groups of least three but no more than seven people. First, work individually by writing your answers to the questions. Then, as a group, discuss everyone's answers. Be prepared to share your answers with other groups.

The First Step: Observing Staff

1. What are places where you could easily be observed by youths?

2. What are some personal things that you have recently discussed on the job within earshot of youths?

3. What are some of your nonverbal tendencies that may be considered extreme tendencies?

The Second Step: Selecting a Victim

4. What type of personal information might you share with youth?

5. When is it permissible to discuss your personal life with a youth?

The Third Step: Setting-Up

6. What is the appropriate action if your favorite youth asks for special permission?

7. When should you notify coworkers or supervisors that a youth has asked for special treatment?

8. How can you tell if a youth has isolated you from other staff members?

9. If isolated, how could you rejoin with other staff members to heal the split?

The Fourth Step: A Seemingly Unimportant Event

10. Why does open communication with coworkers and supervisors stop a seemingly unimportant event?

11. What are some rules that you consider less important but nevertheless enforce?

How to Prevent Delinquent Games

Prevention is the best way to defuse delinquent games. In order to avoid being a victim in a delinquent game, use the two following techniques:

1. **Develop a professional identity:** Develop a professional identity that you show only at work. Reserve your personal identity for friends and family.

2. **Set and maintain boundaries:** A boundary is a division between two entities. You must set and maintain a boundary between you and the youths that you work with. These boundaries are part of your professional identity; only let youths know you as a professional, not as your family and friends know you. You must recognize when you shift from one identity to the other (i.e., when you are no longer maintaining your professional identity but revealing your personal identity).

You will naturally want to respond to youth in your care similar to how you would to your family and friends. Furthermore, you will tend to respond to situations at work similar to how you would in your personal life. However, the youths you supervise are not your family or friends. The youths in confinement are in a special social setting with different social rules. In this setting, relying on personal tendencies can get you into trouble.

A professional is a person who has developed an identity based upon training and professional experience that is separate from his or her personal identity. A professional can drop her or his personal identity at the door and, at work, assume a professional identity.

In the space below, list some topics that you could reveal about yourself at work and topics that would not reveal at work. Use the differences to characterize your professional identity.

Boundary Issue	Professional Identity
Topics I could reveal about myself at work:	
Topics that I would not reveal about myself at work:	

How to Overcome Delinquent Games

You have learned a great deal about delinquent games and how to overcome them. Now, it is time to put it all together. Here are 10 helpful hints for overcoming delinquent games:

1. Do not keep secrets between yourself and a youth.
2. Do not talk about personal issues with youth.
3. Do not talk about personal issues within earshot of youth.
4. Report persona rule violations to your supervisor.
5. When you experience a crisis in your personal life, let your supervisor know.
6. Resolve conflicts with coworkers.
7. Have another staff person near you when dealing with youth.
8. Do not let youth do favors for you.
9. Do not do favors for youth.
10. Do not reveal which youth you prefer.

Role Play Case Scenarios

1. A coworker asks you about your significant other (e.g., spouse, boyfriend, etc.). You notice that you are in earshot of youth. How do you handle the situation?

2. A youth tells you that his uncle has died and asks you to pray with him or her. In the process, the youth asks whether you believe in God and whether you have ever had a loved one die.

3. A youth approaches you and asks you if you can help him or her better understand the dorm rules. As you explain the rules, the youth begins to ask you personal questions. How do you respond?

4. While you are walking from the infirmary to the dorm, a youth tells you that you are his or her favorite staff member. The youth then asks you whether he or she can tell you something that would you have to keep a secret. How do you respond?

How Delinquent Environments Develop

The word *environment* here refers to social environment. A delinquent environment is one in which the youths are in charge, not the staff members. In a delinquent environment, though youth may pretend that they support program rules and prosocial values, these pretensions are false fronts. Behind the false front of compliance, youths act in a delinquent manner. Cliques or gangs form that control the thoughts, feelings, and behaviors of all youth in the dorm. Since staff members cannot control the youth, the youth feel unsafe and, consequently, they act-out.

A delinquent environment can develop in several ways. One common way is described as follows:

Day	Event
Day 1	The youth arrives at the unit. He or she scans the other youth for familiar faces from his or her neighborhood and/or prior incarcerations. The youth also begins to size up staff members and determine each member's characteristics.
Day 3	The youth has made some friends. He or she is a smart, strong person and has thus attracted followers, who he or she spends time getting to know. The youth continues to watch and categorize staff members.
Day 5	The youth begins to manipulate and abuse weaker peers in order to display power to his or her followers. The youth cultivates a reputation of being strong and becomes a leader.
Day 6	The leader begins to send his or her followers on 'search-and-destroy' missions to harm peers. When peers confront his or her followers, the leader steps in intimidatingly and aggressively. The leader consequently confirms his or her strength and teaches both peers and followers that such strength extends to followers.
Day 7	More peers join the leader's clique or gang, which targets positive peers for abuse and for treatment as outcasts.

Day 8	The leader convinces followers to test the power of the staff by sending them on 'search-and-destroy' missions to abuse staff members. The youth enjoys having two groups of followers go on separate missions at the same time.
Day 9	The staff cannot control the leader, and it becomes impossible to comply with the program schedule. At the same time, all youth become openly defiant with staff. The leader becomes intoxicated with power and begins abusing staff and peers in a sadistic manner.

In the example above, a delinquent environment is shown to develop over a period of 9 days following a new youth's entrance into the program. However, it may take more than 9 days for a delinquent environment to develop. By the same token, a delinquent environment could develop more rapidly (i.e., in only 4 or 5 days).

Some delinquent environments develop when two negative leaders form rival cliques or gangs in order to compete with each other for power. The leaders try to recruit more followers than the other. One way to recruit followers is to defy staff and appear to be both a strong conduct disordered youth figure. When two leaders vie for power, the dorm is at great risk for violent acting out.

In the example above, the negative leader is a new youth. However, experience has shown that youth who have been in the program for as few as one and as many as three months may attempt becoming a negative leader. So, it is not only new youth who try to create a delinquent environment.

Regardless of how a delinquent environment develops, it must be stopped. The best way to stop a delinquent environment is to use a large group.

Large Groups

In a residential facility, the entire dorm may convene for a variety of reasons (e.g., to receive mail, for recreation, and to listen to announcements). The type of large group discussed here is not for use except as a behavior management technique.

The large group is used for the same purposes of a huddle-up: to interrupt and confront disruptive youth. Unlike the huddle-up, however, the large group involves all youth in the dorm, while a huddle-up is typically conducted with only a portion of youth in the dorm.

Conducting a Large Group

1. **Preplan the entire process**
    i.   All staff members who will participate should be called together. Since all youth will be participating, it might be necessary to summons staff members from other shifts.
    ii. During the meeting, staff should identify the positive youth in the dorm, as well as the youth who are the negative influences.
    iii. Staff members should diagnosis the source of the problem by asking questions such as, "Are the youth in the dorm merely testing limits?" "Are there competing cliques in the dorm?" and "Does a particular youth serve as a negative leader, and are the other youth following his or her directions?"
    iv. Depending on the diagnosis, staff members should set a specific goal.
    v.   Consideration should also be given to the timeframe for conducting the large group, since large groups can last over a long period of time (e.g., 6 to 20 hours).
    vi. Plans for the youths' school, meal, and recreation schedules must be made.

2. **Form a seed group**
    i.   All youth should be secured in their rooms.
    ii. Assemble all staff and positive youth. It is best to have about six or seven positive youth in the seed group.

iii. Begin by telling the positive youth that the dorm is not safe and that the staff are going to take control. Tell them that they have been identified as positive youth whose help will be enlisted to make the dorm safe again. Let them know that their job is to *give and receive help.*

iv. Tell them that you expect them to confront their peers, especially the negative ones. Explain that before they can confront these negative peers, they must be accountable for their own misconduct.

v. Have each youth explain how he or she has contributed to the problem. Get a commitment from the positive youth to act properly (i.e., to *give and receive help*). After you complete this task, take a break.

3. **Second Wave**

i. Have each positive youth in the seed group pick one peer who they think could help them in gaining control of the dorm.

ii. Reconvene the original seed group with the additional youth selected by members of the seed group.

iii. Begin to turn over control of the group to the seed group members. Have them explain to the new members that there are going to be major changes and that the positive youth are going to control the dorm, not the negative ones.

iv. The new members of the group must do as the seed group members have done; they must identify how they have been part of the problem and indicate how they will be part of the solution in the future.

v. New members must discuss how they will *give and receive help.*

vi. Finally, once all youth have committed to *giving and receiving help*, have the youth plan to confront the negative peers. At this time, over half the dorm should be in the positive group.

4. **Confront the Negative Followers**

i. Assemble all youth and staff in the dayroom, except the youth(s) you think are the negative leaders.

ii. A staff member should explain to the negative youth the process used with their positive peers. The staff member should explain that the positive youth have something to discuss with their negative peers.

    iii.   Staff members should allow positive youth to confront their negative followers and elicit from these negative youth(s) the same discussion that occurred with the positive ones in prior sessions. Negative youths are expected to confess how they have been negative and disruptive, as well as discuss how they will be positive in the future by *giving and receiving help.*

5. **Confront the Negative Leaders**

    i.   After the negative followers have been converted to the good side, bring in the youth(s) who are the negative leaders. You may want to bring in the negative leaders one at a time.

    ii.   Have the entire peer group confront the negative leader(s) and elicit a promise to reform from the negative leaders.

Meetings need to last for as long as it takes to reach the goal and may take several hours and overlap shifts. Take breaks every 90 minutes, during which youth must be kept isolated from each other and staff members should discuss and revise strategies. It may be wise to call the parents of negative peers and have them confront their children.

The large group is typically used to deal with issues affecting the safety of all staff and youth in a dorm (e.g., cliques or gangs have formed, a strong negative leader has gained control of the dorm, there is widespread program disruption, and/or youth have indicated that they do not feel safe).

Perhaps the most difficult type of large group involves confronting a negative leader or a clique or gang. For these large groups, youth living in the dorm are divided into those who have power and those who do not. Your job is wrestle power away from the negative leaders and restore it to the staff and positive youth.

If you are defusing a negative leader or a clique, the strategy of the large group is as follows:

1. Isolate the negative leader from his or her followers.
2. Empower the positive youth.
3. Use the positive youth to confront the negative leader's followers.
4. Make the followers' values and attitudes prosocial.

5. Bring the negative leader back to the group and use all youth, including former followers, to confront the negative leader.

One of the most critical times occurs after a successful large group in which the power has been wrestled away from a negative leader. It is difficult to give up power. So, don't be surprised if the negative leader has difficulty giving up power. In other words, expect the negative leader to try to get revenge or try to reform his or her power base. If this happens, reform the large group and confront the negative leader. After a while, the youths on the dorm will become so fed up with the negative leader for making them go to large group that the negative leader will not be able to form a power base.

Shut-Downs

A shut-down occurs when the staff locks the youth in their rooms because all or most youth are acting out and there is a widespread threat to the welfare of the youths and staff. A shut-down is the most restrictive behavior management technique anyone can use and it should only be used as a last resort.

Perhaps the most common—and most detrimental—mistakes made when conducting a shut-down stem from becoming isolated from other staff members. If a shut-down is done correctly, it is a time of intense, direct interaction between the staff and youth.

Criteria for a Shut-Down

1. Pervasive and serious threat to the welfare of staff and youth;
2. Less restrictive interventions have failed;
3. Serious acting out appears imminent.

Conducting a Shut-Down

1. After the criteria for a shut-down have been met, the shut-down must be approved by administrators.
2. Preplan the entire process. If necessary, increase the number of staff members on duty. Arrange for school, meal, and recreation schedules to be conducted in the dorm.
3. Put all youth in their rooms. Go from room to room and outline the expectations and behavioral goals that youth must meet before being released.
4. Assign the following roles to staff members:
   a) *Investigator*: interviews youth to uncover information
   b) *Monitor*: Observes youth in rooms
   c) *Educator*: Retrains youth on orientation material.
5. Each youth should have contact with at least one staff member per shift, even the nighttime shift.

6. Youth who meet criteria can be released from their rooms with probation status. These youth are allowed to work on assignments in the dayroom and have more privileges than youth in their rooms. When possible, these youth should be involved in at least one behavior group per day.

7. Continue the shut-down process until the dorm environment is safe. It may be necessary to conduct a large group at some point during the process.

Target Behaviors

Each youth you supervise will have a treatment plan. The treatment plan specifies the target behaviors a youth must address to reach their goal of **No More Victims**.

You can help a youth work on rehabilitation issues by knowing the target behaviors and helping the youth recognize and control them.

In the Limit & Lead Program, there are five categories of target behaviors. A youth should always be working on ways to eliminate or control behavior that falls into these categories.

1. **Criminal orientation:** Use of delinquent skills and failure to develop or use citizen skills.

2. **Thinking errors:** Thoughts that leads to acting out, including criminal outlets, criminal precursors, and crimes.

3. **Poor coping ability with unpleasant emotions:** Responding to triggers and stress with one of the three unpleasant emotions: fear, anger, or sadness.

4. **Poor self-management:** Unwillingness or inability to use self-control. When a youth acts out because of poor self-management, others must step in and control the youth.

5. **Having conduct disordered youth friends and associates:** The youth seeks out delinquents as friends, or he or she seeks friends who won't interfere with acting out behavior.

It should be clear why direct care staff and security staff should monitor target behaviors. If a youth is benefiting from the Limit & Lead Rehabilitation Program, then he or she should rely less and less on target behaviors over the course of treatment. Anything that direct care staff and security staff do to help the youths eliminate these behaviors helps the youths get closer to the goal of **No More Victims**.

Helping Youths reduce Target Behaviors

If a youth wants to reach the goal of **No More Victims**, he or she must show improvement in all five target behaviors. Like anyone else, if a youth sets goals, he or she is more likely to succeed.

When youth set goals to overcome target behavior, we don't just ask them to avoid using target behaviors. We ask them to develop positive, prosocial behaviors to replace the target behaviors.

Asking the youth to develop positive behaviors to replace target behaviors is using a principle known as *response competition*: a youth can't be doing something bad if he or she is already doing something good. Consider the five target behaviors. Here are some ideas about the opposite of each:

Target Behavior	Replacement Behavior	Examples of Replacement Behavior
Criminal orientation	Citizen orientation	1. Follows rules and laws. 2. Supports other citizens. 3. Confronts criminal behavior.
Thinking errors	Thinking like a citizen	1. Agrees with laws and rules. 2. Develops a personal code of behavior befitting a citizen. 3. Shows altruism by working for the good of others
Poor social and emotional skills	Positive social and emotional skills	1. Can recognize and control negative emotions. 2. Can express and resolve negative emotions. 3. Can help others to deal with their emotional issues.

Poor self-management	Good self-management	1. Plans and considers consequences before acting.
		2. Develops long-term plans
		3. Can care for self and meet basic needs.
Conduct disordered youth influences	Positive influences	1. Avoids criminals.
		2. Seeks out positive peers.
		3. Positively influences others.

Take a close look at the behaviors listed in the third column. These behaviors are arranged in terms of difficulty; behaviors listed at the top of the list are more easily performed than behaviors underneath.

You can use this hierarchy to help youths set goals. Youths new to the program should be asked to set simpler goals but youths who have been here a while should show progress by reaching more challenging goals.

As a staff member who supervises youth, your job is to help them to exhibit positive behaviors. You should encourage them to engage in any behavior that prevents them from engaging in a target behavior.

Characteristics of Effective Staff who Work Effectively
with Conduct Disordered Youth

Not everyone is cut out to work with conduct disordered youth. Some people are very effective with these youths, while others are ineffective. There is much at risk when an ineffective person works with conduct disordered youth because when these youth act out, they hurt others. If you realize that you are not cut out to work with conduct disordered youths, then seek another line of work.

To determine if you have what it takes to effectively work with these youth, consider the following list of characteristics of effective staff members as they pertain to the profession:

Commitment   You must have a personal desire to work with conduct disordered youths. You should derive intrinsic reward from your work and not rely on reward from the conduct disordered youth.

Responsibility When you work with conduct disordered youth, you have to show them you are responsible if you are going to teach them how to be responsible. If you have difficulty being responsible, don't work with conduct disordered youth.

Intensity   You must be passionate about your work. It takes passion and intensity to work with any youth, especially conduct disordered youths. If you are just here for the paycheck, it is only a matter of time before bad things will happen to you.

Skepticism   You must be able to tolerate ambiguity, i.e., not knowing the answer. You should not accept answers, especially verbal answers, given by youth. You should be willing to postpone conclusions and continue probing.

Leadership   Youth follow people who lead. You must have leadership skills. You must be comfortable with leading youth toward adopting citizen-oriented ways of life.

Common problems associated with working with conduct disordered youth are listed below. It is possible to overcome any of these problems. However, if you have repeatedly tried to overcome these problems and cannot, you may not be cut out for working with conduct disordered youth.

Permissiveness: You are permissive if you don't give consequences for acting out. Permissive staff members tend be intimidated by youth and these feelings of intimidation are often the basis for not giving consequences. Sometimes, permissive staff are really very aggressive and they don't confront because they fear if they start confronting they will lose control and become aggressive. Behavior typical of permissive staff members includes:

1. Rationalizing how to avoid giving consequences to youth who act out;
2. Recommending that consequences, punishment, and negative reinforcement not be used;
3. Theorizing that conduct disordered youth harmless or misguided;
4. Making colleagues feel guilty for enforcing rules.

Harshness: You are harsh when you overreact or use excessive punishment. The harsh staff person is often intimidated by youth and typically project their own aggressive impulses onto youth. Behavior typical of harsh staff members includes:

1. Failing to show compassion for youth;
2. Developing punitive programs that do not afford the youth the chance to develop self-esteem;
3. Being unwilling to lift restrictions, even when a youth overcomes target behavior;
4. Using a formal system of consequences to break the youth's spirit;
5. Using a formal system of consequences for revenge;
6. Reporting that he or she has never been conned or manipulated by the youth; and,
7. Placing himself or herself in dangerous situations with youth and refusing to recognize the anger.

So, here is the bottom line: Very Few Individuals Are Cutout to Work with Conduct Disordered Youth.

If you are one of the few who will work effectively with these youth, then congratulations! You have found job that could become your calling.

If you are not cutout for working effectively with conduct disordered youth, do not step foot on the dorm. Quit now, before you or someone else gets hurt.

www.ingramcontent.com/pod-product-compliance
Lightning Source LLC
Chambersburg PA
CBHW080424290526
45791CB00008BA/2399